Step Outside

written and illustrated by
doretta groenendyk

The Acorn Press
Charlottetown
2013

ACORNPRESS

P.O. Box 22024
Charlottetown, Prince Edward Island
C1A 9J2
acornpresscanada.com

Editing by Sherie Hodds
Cover and interior design by Matt Reid
Typeface based on hand writing by Doretta
Bike drawings by Jasper
Printed in Canada

Library and Archives Canada Cataloguing in Publication

Groenendyk, Doretta, author
Step outside / Doretta Groenendyk.

ISBN 978-1-927502-19-8 (bound)

1. Outdoor recreation--Juvenile literature. I. Title.

GV191.62.G76 2013   j796.083   C2013-904724-7

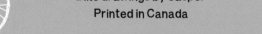

Canada ▮♦▮   ❀ Canada Council   Conseil des Arts
                for the Arts   du Canada

The publisher acknowledges the support of the Government of Canada through the Canada Book Fund of the Department of Canadian Heritage and the Canada Council for the Arts Block Grant Program.

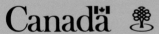

Arts
NOVA SCOTIA
NOUVELLE-ÉCOSSE

The artist wishes to thank the Nova Scotia Government Department of Communities, Culture and Heritage for their support.

for david, jasper, izra, reilly,
lulu, nutnut and poppy

Hide in shadows
under the moon.

Discover the world in which you live.

And travel through the

space between.

Hey you! Yes YOU!

sense

dreams

Step outside with outside friends.

Visit sounds and drift away.

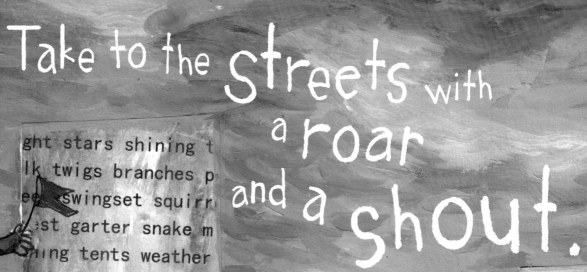

Take to the **streets** with a **roar** and a **shout.**

Footprint

again

Or wander through.

The world on foot holds a promise for you.

EXPLORE

sleep
below stars
and wake by the sun.